GIANT PANDAS

BY NANCY FURSTINGER

Published by The Child's World®
1980 Lookout Drive • Mankato, MN 56003-1705
800-599-READ • www.childsworld.com

Acknowledgments
The Child's World®: Mary Berendes, Publishing Director
Red Line Editorial: Editorial direction and production
The Design Lab: Design
Amnet: Production

Design Element: Shutterstock Images
Photographs ©: nelik/iStock/Thinkstock, cover, 1;
Hung Chung Chih/Shutterstock Images, 4, 13,
16, 22; View Stock/Thinkstock, 5; Donyanedomam/
iStockphoto, 7; irakite/Shutterstock Images, 8; enmyo/
Shutterstock Images, 10; zhuweiyi49/iStockphoto, 11;
Takahashi Kei/iStockphoto, 15; Gang Liu/Shutterstock
Images, 17; ChinaTopix/AP Images, 18–19;
ChameleonsEye/Shutterstock Images, 21

ISBN 9781631439698
LCCN 2014959639

Printed in the United States of America
Mankato, MN
July, 2015
PA02264

ABOUT THE AUTHOR

Nancy Furstinger has been speaking up for animals since she learned to talk. She is the author of nearly 100 books, including many on her favorite topic: animals! She shares her home with big dogs and house rabbits (all rescued). Furstinger also volunteers for several animal organizations.

TABLE OF CONTENTS

CHAPTER ONE

GIANT BEAR CATS

Giant pandas spend much of their time eating.

A giant panda sits in a bamboo tree. The black-and-white

bear tears off bamboo branches. It eats the leaves and tender

shoots. Giant pandas are the stars in zoos around the world.

But today only approximately 1,600 live in the mountains of

China. Giant pandas are **endangered** in the wild. They are at high risk of becoming **extinct** unless people help.

The Chinese call pandas "giant bear cats." But they are not cats. Pandas are a **rare** type of bear. They are about the size of an American black bear. Males weigh up to 250 pounds (113 kg). Females weigh up to 220 pounds (100 kg). The pandas stand 2.5 feet (0.8 m) tall at the shoulders and are 5 feet (1.5 m) long.

Pandas live in the cool, wet forests of central China.

Pandas live in six mountain ranges in central China. The mountains rise 5,000 to 10,000 feet (1,525 to 3,050 m). On the mountainsides, cool and wet forests are hidden in clouds. These forests are the giant panda's **habitat**.

Pandas eat mostly one type of plant. Their diet is 99 percent bamboo. They can spend 16 hours a day eating. Bamboo is low in **nutrients**. That is why pandas must eat plenty. They eat approximately 28 pounds (13 kg) each day. That is the same weight as 180 ice cream sandwiches. Pandas also eat grasses and sometimes **rodents**. Pandas do not store much fat from their diet. So they do not **hibernate** like other bears. Luckily for the pandas, bamboo is available year-round.

Pandas are built to grab and chomp bamboo. They have a sixth finger on their front paws. This stubby finger grows

KEEPING IN TOUCH

*Pandas mostly live alone. But they keep in touch with other pandas. Pandas bark, honk, huff, and growl. Male and female pandas also mark trees. They leave stinky messages using scent **glands** under their tails. Males may even do handstands to leave scent marks high up on trees.*

out of the panda's wrist. It acts as a thumb. Pandas grasp bamboo with their six fingers. They use strong jaws and 42 teeth to crush and chew tough bamboo.

Pandas have huge heads and chunky bodies. They have rounded ears and short tails. Thick fur covers pandas in layers. Their outer coat feels oily. Water runs off this fur to keep pandas dry. Their undercoat feels like wool. It keeps

Pandas use their stubby sixth finger to grasp bamboo.

Pandas have distinctive black-and-white fur.

pandas warm. Black patches circle pandas' eyes. Black also covers their ears, arms, legs, and shoulders. The rest of their fur is snowy white. Scientists believe the colors help pandas. They can blend in with bamboo, rocks, and snow.

Giant panda females give birth every two years. Newborn pandas are very tiny. A **cub** can weigh 4 to 6 ounces (113 to 170 g). That is about the same as a stick of butter.

Each cub is only 6 inches (15 cm) long. Babies are born blind and with pink skin and white fur. After two weeks, they grow black patches of fur. They begin to look like adult pandas.

Mother pandas raise their cubs inside dens. Some dens are hidden inside caves. Others are in hollow tree stumps. A panda cub lives with its mother for up to two-years. Then the

Giant pandas go through a lot of changes in their first year of life.

newborn

one week old

three weeks old

three months old

six months old

one year old

**Panda cubs stay with their mothers for the
first two years of their lives.**

mother sends her cub away so she can raise her next baby.

Pandas live about 20 years in the wild. Zoo pandas can live

up to 35 years.

Giant pandas are designed to live in the wild. But today

their bamboo forests are being cut down. Pandas are in

danger of disappearing from China.

CHAPTER TWO

LOSS OF HABITAT

As people clear land, pandas are pushed higher into the mountains.

Pandas once lived in the lowlands around the Yangtze River. But panda habitat has shrunk. More people live in China than in any other country. These people need a lot of land to live. They cleared the land to grow crops and build homes. Pandas were pushed out of the lowlands. They went higher into the mountains.

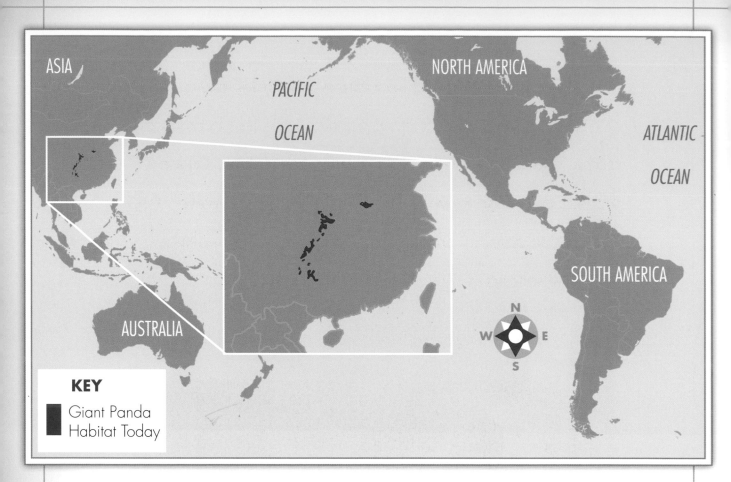

Giant panda habitat in China is shrinking.

But pandas' mountain homes are also threatened. People clear the forests for wood and fuel. They chop down the bamboo pandas need. People use bamboo as a building material. They also eat bamboo shoots. Loggers build roads and railroads that crisscross the mountain forests. This keeps pandas apart and prevents them from finding mates.

Female pandas become mothers when they are around four to eight years old. Mother pandas have few cubs. Each mother raises only five to eight cubs in her lifetime. Panda mothers give birth to twins about half the time. However, the mother can care for only one cub. She picks the healthiest one. The second cub usually does not survive.

It is rare for panda mothers to care for two cubs at a time.

Some animals hunt panda cubs. Tigers and leopards are rare in the wild. But they are still deadly panda **predators**. Weasels, Asian golden cats, and Asian wild dogs called dholes all hunt panda cubs.

Few predators attack adult pandas. Pandas climb trees to stay safe. Most of the time, pandas move slowly. But they can run up to 20 miles per hour (32 kmh) to escape danger.

Bamboo die-offs are a greater problem for pandas. The bears eat more than 40 **species** of bamboo. This woody plant is the fastest-growing plant in the world. It flowers and drops its seeds every 20 to 40 years. Then all the plants of that species die off. The bamboo will not grow back for another four to ten years.

Bamboo die-offs were not a problem in the past. Pandas would move to another area with a bamboo forest.

POACHING PANDAS

Poachers illegally hunt pandas. Black-and-white panda *pelts* sell for approximately $10,000 in Asia. Panda poachers face 20 years in prison if caught. This stiff penalty cuts down on poaching. But pandas also get caught in traps set for other animals, such as musk deer.

Today, however, pandas have been forced into smaller pockets of space. They can no longer freely move to another bamboo forest. Sometimes pandas starve when bamboo starts dying off.

Earthquakes also affect bamboo. Earthquakes are common in China. The shaking of Earth's crust causes bamboo to start flowering. Then it dies off before completing its growing cycle. Without bamboo, pandas will not survive.

Bamboo forests are important for giant panda survival.

CHAPTER THREE

NATURE RESERVES

People in China protect panda habitat by creating nature reserves.

People in China and across the world work to protect pandas.
Nature **reserves** help pandas survive. These areas of land
are set aside to protect panda habitat. China has more than
50 panda reserves. They cover nearly four million acres
(1.6 million ha) of forest. China is also building sections of
bamboo forest to connect the reserves.

Some reserves have research centers where scientists study panda behavior. The Wolong Nature Reserve was the first to start a program to **breed** pandas in 1981. It is called the Wolong Panda Center. Scientists there help panda mothers raise twins. They trade cubs back and forth so both babies get equal care. Cub survival has tripled at the reserve.

In 2008 an earthquake destroyed the Wolong Panda Center. Pregnant mother pandas were the first to be safely moved. They all gave birth to healthy cubs. China rebuilt the Wolong Panda Center. It built other panda nurseries, too.

Panda cubs enjoy some bamboo at the Wolong Panda Center.

Panda reserves also return pandas to the wild. Panda cubs start wilderness training at around two months old. They are placed in a large wild area protected by fences. Scientists use hidden cameras to watch the cubs.

Scientists wear giant panda costumes whenever they check on cubs. They weigh the cubs and give them exams. Scientists do not want the cubs to lose their fear of humans. Scientists even smear their costumes with panda dung. This hides their human scent. Scientists teach panda

Panda researchers wear panda costumes when handling cubs.

cubs how to live on their own. Pandas get lessons on how to find food. They also learn how to choose a safe spot to sleep.

Zoos also run panda breeding programs. In 1999 San Diego Zoo Global made a deal with China. In return for money, the San Diego Zoo got to display two pandas for 12 years. One panda, Bai Yun, gave birth to six cubs during that time. Her first cub traveled to China. She entered a breeding program there. She gave birth to ten more cubs.

Pandas are one of the most popular zoo animals. Chicago's Brookfield Zoo was the first in the world to display a panda. The zoo bought Su-Lin for around $9,000 in 1937. The cub drew more visitors than any other animal in the zoo's history.

Today China loans pandas to zoos around the world. Zoos pay a fee for each year they display pandas. Much of

PANDA PLAYGROUND

Playful pandas need a playground to exercise their bodies and brains. Zoos build jungle gyms for pandas to climb. Pandas also splash in pools. They play with toys, such as balls, barrels, and dumbbells. They eat special panda ice pops. They are made out of fruit frozen inside chunks of ice.

the money is used to protect pandas in the wild. The fee supports nature reserves in China. Visitors help save giant pandas in the wild whenever they buy tickets to the zoo.

Pandas are China's national treasure. Humans need to protect these giant bear cats. Then future generations of pandas will roam the wild.

People around the world visit zoos to see giant pandas.

WHAT YOU CAN DO

- "Adopt" a giant panda at a panda reserve in China. Select a panda to sponsor from Pandas International. The group will send a photo of your adopted panda along with updates.

- Visit a zoo with a giant panda exhibit. Your admission ticket helps to save this endangered species in the wild.

- Brainstorm Chinese names for pandas when they are born at a zoo. Many zoos host naming contests. Then spread the word about why these black-and-white bears need to be protected in their natural habitat.

GLOSSARY

breed (BREED) To breed is to keep animals so that they can produce more young. Scientists breed giant pandas.

cub (KUB) A cub is a very young bear. A panda cub starts crawling at around ten weeks of age.

endangered (en-DANE-jerd) An endangered animal is in danger of becoming extinct. Giant pandas are endangered.

extinct (ek-STINKT) If a type of animal is extinct, all the animals have died out. Without help, pandas may become extinct.

glands (GLANDZ) Glands are cells that release materials, such as scent, from the body. Pandas use their scent glands to communicate with one another.

habitat (HAB-i-tat) A habitat is a place where an animal lives. Panda habitat is shrinking.

hibernate (HIE-bur-nayt) To hibernate is to pass a length of time in a resting state. Pandas do not hibernate like other bear species.

nutrients (NOO-tree-ents) Nutrients are substances living things need to grow and be healthy. Bamboo is low in nutrients.

pelts (PELTS) Pelts are animal skins. Panda pelts are sold in Asia.

poachers (PO-churz) Poachers are people who illegally hunt and kill animals. Poachers kill pandas.

predators (PRED-a-terz) Predators hunt, kill, and eat other animals. Pandas have few predators in the wild.

rare (RARE) If something is rare, it is uncommon. Pandas are very rare.

reserves (ree-ZURVZ) Reserves are protected areas. China has created nature reserves for giant pandas.

rodents (RO-dents) Rodents are small animals with fur and sharp teeth. Pandas sometimes eat rodents.

shoots (SHOOTS) Shoots are young branches. Giant pandas eat bamboo shoots.

species (SPEE-sheez) A species is a group of animals or plants that are similar and can produce offspring. There are more than 40 species of bamboo.

TO LEARN MORE

BOOKS

Buller, Laura. *The Great Panda Tale*. New York: DK Publishing, 2014.

Lai, Fanny. *A Visual Celebration of Giant Pandas*.
Singapore: Editions Didier Millet, 2012.

Schreiber, Anne. *Pandas*. Washington, DC: National Geographic, 2010.

WEB SITES

Visit our Web site for links about giant pandas:
childsworld.com/links

Note to Parents, Teachers, and Librarians: We routinely verify our Web links to make sure they are safe and active sites. So encourage your readers to check them out!

INDEX